D1311271

CORE SKILLS

EXPRESS IT
SHARING YOUR
MEDIA ONLINE

Gillian Gosman

PowerKiDS
press.
New York

Published in 2015 by The Rosen Publishing Group, Inc.
29 East 21st Street, New York, NY 10010

First Edition

Editor: Caitie McAneney
Book Design: Mickey Harmon

Photo Credits: Cover (picture) Samuel Borges Photography/Shutterstock.com; cover (background) Attitude/Shutterstock.com; pp. 3–5, 6–10, 12–20, 22–32 (dot backgrounds) vlastas/Shutterstock.com; p. 5 Jamie Grill/The Image Bank/Getty Images; p. 6 Ruslan Guzov/Shutterstock.com; p. 7 Rob Marmion/Shutterstock.com; p. 9 Mila May/Shutterstock.com; p. 11 AVAVA/Shutterstock.com; p. 13 (boy with camera) Denis Kuvaev/Shutterstock.com; p. 13 (scanner) pryzmat/Shutterstock.com; p. 14 wavebreakmedia/Shutterstock.com; p. 15 (laptop) artjazz/Shutterstock.com; p. 15 (camera) Joel_420/Shutterstock.com; p. 17 (jumping) Jacek Chabraszewski/Shutterstock.com; p. 17 (girl) Enrico Fianchini/E+/Getty Images; p. 18 Pete Pahham/Shutterstock.com; p. 19 racorn/Shutterstock.com; p. 21 jannoon028/Shutterstock.com; p. 23 (hands) Dragon Images/Shutterstock.com; p. 23 (girl) Maryna Kulchytska/Shutterstock.com; p. 25 ZouZou/Shutterstock.com; p. 26 Basileus/Shutterstock.com; p. 27 Oksana Kuzmina/Shutterstock.com; p. 29 Peter Dazeley/Stone/Getty Images; p. 30 stockyimages/Shutterstock.com.

Library of Congress Cataloging-in-Publication Data

Gosman, Gillian.
 Express it : sharing your media online / Gillian Gosman.
     pages cm. — (Core skills)
 Includes index.
ISBN 978-1-4777-7394-9 (pbk.)
ISBN 978-1-4777-7395-6 (6 pack)
ISBN 978-1-4777-7393-2 (library binding)
1. Computer file sharing—Juvenile literature. 2. Multimedia systems—Juvenile literature. 3. Online social networks—Juvenile literature. I. Title.
 QA76.9.F5G685 2015
 006.7—dc23
                                    2014036229

Manufactured in the United States of America

CPSIA Compliance Information: Batch #CW15PK: For Further Information contact Rosen Publishing, New York, New York at 1-800-237-9932

CONTENTS

Sharing Digital Media 4

Why Share? 6

What Are Digital Tools? 8

Social Media and Classroom Tools 10

Sharing Photographs 12

Making Videos and Sharing 16

Infographics 20

How to Collaborate Online 24

Fit to Share? 26

Staying Safe Online 28

Express Yourself! 30

Glossary 31

Index 32

Websites 32

SHARING DIGITAL MEDIA

The Internet provides many tools for creating and sharing information with friends and strangers near and far. In today's world, it's easy to share digital **media**. Digital media can refer to anything created, viewed, edited, or shared on a computer. This includes photographs, **audio**, text, and videos.

We share digital media through a variety of platforms, which are websites and programs that host content created by users. For example, blog platforms host people's writing. Video platforms, such as YouTube (youtube.com), host people's videos. The type of platform we choose depends on the kind of digital media we want to share, our **audience**, and how much we want to pay to store our media online.

QUICK TIP

The phrase "digital media" is meant to set computer-based media apart from older forms of media, such as television, radio, and newspaper.

What kind of media would you like to make? If you're a musician, you might like to create audio or video files. If you're an artist, you might like to upload photographs and artwork you've created.

WHY SHARE?

People share digital media for a variety of reasons. They may want to inform others about something, such as a charity or a scientific discovery. They may want to entertain people with funny writing or videos.

There are many reasons for young people to share media. Sometimes students are asked to **collaborate** on the creation of digital media for schoolwork. They may want to stay in touch with friends and family or share their interests and hobbies with those around them.

Whether you're sharing digital media for a school project or with family, it's important to learn the tools of the trade and practice safe online behavior. In this book, we'll explore both!

Some people simply enjoy the excitement of receiving feedback about something they've created and shared. The Internet makes it possible for anyone to publish content and then experience the praise and **criticism** of other Internet users. Sometimes criticism can be hard to hear, but it can inspire you to make your work even better!

WHAT ARE DIGITAL TOOLS?

Digital tools are resources and programs that help you create, edit, store, and share your digital media. For example, if you've recorded video on your digital camera or smartphone, you might use a digital editing tool to create a movie. Then you might use another digital tool to share that movie with friends, family members, or classmates.

Imagine you have a presentation for social studies class. You might make your presentation materials using a digital program, such as PowerPoint. You could also choose an online tool, such as Prezi (prezi.com), Glogster (glogster.com), or Google Presentation (docs.google.com/presentation).

QUICK TIP

Some digital tools are free, while others require you to buy them or make an account. Do your **research** to find which tools are best for you.

What if you have a writing assignment for language arts? You might choose to create an eBook, or a digital text, using a tool such as the Mac Book Creator **application** for tablets.

Many digital tools come with your laptop or tablet, or they can be bought as an application, or app. For example, many devices come with special programs for making movies and editing pictures.

SOCIAL MEDIA AND CLASSROOM TOOLS

Social media usually refers to websites and online applications that connect people in a network, or a group of people. Social media websites allow users to share content and comment on one another's content. Some of the most common social media websites are Facebook (facebook.com), Twitter (twitter.com), Tumblr (tumblr.com), and YouTube (youtube.com). Social media websites are where many Internet users spend a majority of their time online.

Certain media websites are designed for creating a network within a school or classroom setting. Some websites, such as Gaggle (gaggle.net), help students learn and work together. Websites like Schoology (schoology.com) build a network around a class's assignments and learning resources. These websites make it easy to connect with classmates and share writing, videos, and presentations.

Before you use a media-sharing website for class, be sure you understand and follow your teacher's expectations. Which sites you visit, when you visit them, and how you contribute to the social media conversation should all be appropriate for school.

11

SHARING PHOTOGRAPHS

Do you like taking photographs? What things would you like to capture in a photograph? Some people take photographs of their favorite places. Other people love taking photographs while hanging out with friends.

There are many websites and applications for editing digital photographs, creating **collages**, and sharing these images. First, you need to upload the photograph you would like to share. If the photograph was taken with a device that can connect to the Internet, such as a smartphone, you can upload the image directly to the Internet. Otherwise, you'll need to connect the camera or phone to your computer using a special cord, called a USB cord. Usually, your computer will download the pictures from the camera right away or ask you to choose a computer program to do so.

Many electronic devices can take pictures. You can use a digital camera or smartphone. You can also use a film camera. Some people like using film cameras because they prefer the quality of the photographs. Some enjoy developing the film, or treating it to produce images, and then printing the images by themselves.

QUICK TIP

If you have a picture taken with a film camera, you can capture the image using a **scanner** and save the file to your computer.

Once you have a digital version of the photograph saved on your computer, it's time to create! Consider what you would like to do with your image. Dozens of websites and applications, such as Instagram (instagram.com) and the PicCollage application, offer free picture-editing tools. These tools make it possible for users to change the colors of their image, collect multiple images in a collage, and add stickers, frames, and text.

Sharing photographs can be fun, but make sure you only share things that you and other people will feel good about. For example, don't post embarrassing photographs of someone you know. While it may seem funny, that person probably won't feel the same way.

QUICK TIP

You can also upload your creations to free photo-sharing services, such as Snapfish (snapfish.com), Picasa (picasa.google.com), and Shutterfly (shutterfly.com). If you want to buy copies of your photographs, these websites can produce prints and gifts with your photograph on them. Many photo-sharing websites also have editing features.

Most picture-editing applications have features built in for sharing your images online, either through social networking websites or privately through email and text message. You can share a picture of your vacation with your family. You can also tag a person, or link to their social media account, if you have a picture of them.

MAKING VIDEOS AND SHARING

Another way to share your experiences or express yourself might be through a video. Videos can be entertaining and informative, and they can even be used for school projects and presentations. What would you record in a video? Some people take videos of themselves singing or playing an instrument to show off their skills and gain fans. Some people make instructional videos, such as videos about how to make a craft or bake a cake.

You can record a video using a video camera, digital camera, or smartphone. Video files can be uploaded much like picture files: either over the Internet or through a USB cord. Next, find a video program that fits your needs, such as Windows Movie Maker or iMovie.

QUICK TIP
Video editing programs allow you to drag video clips to a timeline, cut and delete unwanted video, and add audio, text, and other special effects.

My_Movie.mov

	0:0	1:00	2:00
Julia			
Mom			
Effects			
Tommy			

Some programs and applications allow you to place your video into popular formats, such as movie trailers, slide shows, and advertisements.

You've recorded your video and edited it. Now, you want to share it online. To do so, simply create or log on to an account on a video-sharing website or content storage site, such as YouTube (youtube.com) or Vimeo (vimeo.com). Next, upload your videos, following the prompts on the screen. When your video is uploaded, watch it to make sure there are no problems. Then, you can let friends and family know you've posted a video.

QUICK TIP

Brainstorm a few ways you can use videos in your work for school. You could do a video interview to get information or personal stories for a project. You can record a day-in-the-life video of someone with a certain job or make a video educating people on a topic, such as cooking.

If your teacher has assigned a video project, they may choose to share your work on a school-friendly website such as TeacherTube (teachertube.com). This website allows teachers to create digital classrooms with content created by teachers and students.

Some people share short video clips on Vine, which is an application that allows you to share videos through social media websites. However, it's recommended that young people be careful when sharing videos publicly. Make sure the content is appropriate and doesn't give away private information.

INFOGRAPHICS

Infographics are **visual** representations of information. Their purpose is to share information in the most understandable way possible. Tables, graphs, maps, timelines, flow charts, and diagrams are all examples of infographics.

There are many tools online for creating numerical infographics, or those dealing with numbers and other data, such as graphs and tables. The National Center for Education Statistics has an online tool for creating graphs on their Kidz Zone website (http://nces.ed.gov/nceskids/createagraph/). ChartGo (chartgo.com) is a more advanced tool for creating charts and graphs.

Be sure to collect all your data before you begin. Then, enter the information carefully. Finally, save your infographic as an image file so you can upload and share it using social networking websites, classroom websites, or email.

Adding infographics to a project or paper can make it more interesting and easy to understand. Sharing infographics that you've made can help educate people on the data you've collected.

Not all infographics are designed to share numerical data, however. Infographics can also share ideas, thought patterns, events, and connections between words or concepts.

You can use infographics to organize your thoughts while brainstorming. Some applications, such as Inspiration Map and Kidspiration, are **designed** to help you create and share organizers and concept maps. Some applications allow you to add graphics and audio files to your visual. You can share this media with friends, family, and classmates to show them how you organize your information or ideas.

When you're writing a history paper or reading a story, you might want to make a timeline of events. Capzles (capzles.com) and Timeglider (timeglider.com) are online programs for creating interactive timelines, complete with photographs, videos, music, and documents.

Flowcharts are infographics that illustrate the steps in a process. You can upload a flowchart and share it online to teach your friends and family how to do something, such as make cupcakes.

Making Cupcakes

Stir cake mix, eggs, oil, and water together.

▽

Pour ingredients into cupcake pan with cupcake liners.

▽

Place pan in oven for 20 minutes.

▽

Remove cupcakes and let them cool.

▽

Spread frosting on cupcakes.

▽

Decorate!

HOW TO COLLABORATE ONLINE

Working with your classmates on pair and group projects is a great way to develop teamwork skills. Collaborating, or working together, can sometimes be hard, especially when it comes to arranging a time to work. However, it's easy to collaborate online!

Partners and groups can have face-to-face conversations using **video-conferencing** programs, such as Skype (skype.com) or Google Hangouts (plus.google.com/hangouts). These programs can be used on any digital device with a built-in camera and Internet capability.

QUICK TIP

Before you begin collaborating with your group, create and share an online calendar with the important dates for your project. Google Calendar (google.com/calendar) and 30 Boxes (30boxes.com) both offer easy-to-use, free calendars that can be created, shared, and updated. Having a calendar with due dates will help keep everyone on the same page!

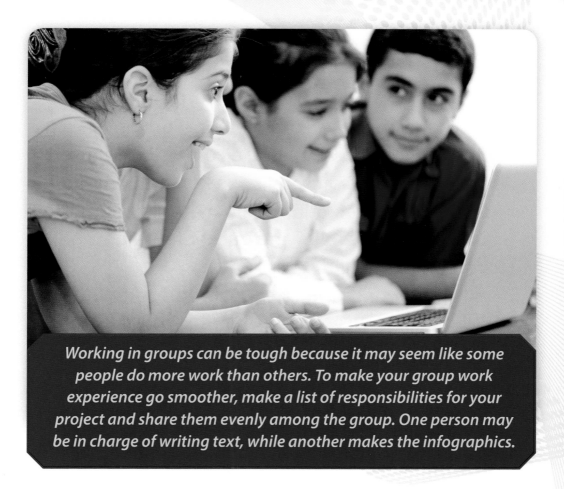

Working in groups can be tough because it may seem like some people do more work than others. To make your group work experience go smoother, make a list of responsibilities for your project and share them evenly among the group. One person may be in charge of writing text, while another makes the infographics.

Students can also make free accounts for storing and sharing content online through websites such as Dropbox (dropbox.com) and Google Drive (drive.google.com). Google Drive allows multiple users to work on a document at the same time on separate computers. These kinds of programs make it easy for everyone in a group to contribute to the work.

FIT TO SHARE?

When you share, comment on, and discuss content online, you're joining a community of users. As with any other community, the online community has rules and expectations for behavior. It's important to ask yourself the following questions before you share, comment, or discuss.

Is your work complete, clean, and edited? Check and double-check your work. Be sure any information you share is true.

QUICK TIP

You may see a picture, watch a video, or find an infographic that was made by someone else and have the urge to share it with your friends. This is usually fine, as long as you give credit to the original creator.

> *It's your responsibility to decide whether the pictures, videos, or infographics you create should be shared with the Internet community. Take this responsibility seriously! Don't share content or comments that are violent or rude.*

Are you making a meaningful, thoughtful contribution? Will your contribution be useful to your audience? If you're sharing a video about making salsa, how can you make it original and useful?

Does your content reflect well on you? Some Internet users post hurtful and inappropriate content to social media websites. Only share content that is kind and considerate.

STAYING SAFE ONLINE

The Internet brings the world to your fingertips, but with that opportunity comes danger. Follow a few simple rules to stay safe online.

Don't use social media websites until you're old enough to do so or you have permission from a parent. Facebook's minimum age is 13. Also, when using social media sites, make your privacy settings as strict as possible. This means the public can't see your personal details or the content you post.

Never share personal information, including your address, phone number, school name, or any other details that could allow someone to determine your location. Never share your passwords with friends or strangers. If you come across anything online that makes you uncomfortable, tell an adult.

QUICK TIP

If you do decide to share content online, create a username that's different from your real name. This will make it harder for strangers to determine your real identity.

Remember that people are not always who they say they are online, and someone might be using a fake identity. Never arrange to meet someone in person whom you know only through the Internet without an adult's knowledge and presence.

EXPRESS YOURSELF!

Digital tools are transforming the ways we communicate with people. They make it easier than ever to express your creativity to your networks through pictures, videos, and infographics. Are you interested in nature? You can take photographs of landscapes and animals and upload them to share online. Are you interested in playing piano? You can take videos of yourself playing piano and share them to gain fans.

The more you explore digital tools, the more useful these tools will be. We've taken a look at many websites, programs, and applications in this book. However, digital resources are constantly changing, so you can discover many more resources and choose the ones that work for you. Get ready to learn, create, and share!

GLOSSARY

application (aa-pluh-KAY-shun) A program used on a computer or device that does a certain task.

audience (AW-dee-uhns) A group of people who see, hear, or read something.

audio (AW-dee-oh) Having to do with sound.

collaborate (kuh-LAA-buh-rayt) To work jointly toward a common goal.

collage (kuh-LAHZH) A collection of pictures in one image.

criticism (KRIH-tuh-sih-zuhm) The judgment of both the good and bad qualities of a work of art or literature.

design (dih-ZYN) To plan the way something will look or work.

media (MEE-dee-uh) The means of communication that reach or influence many people.

research (REE-surch) The act of studying to find something new.

scanner (SKAA-nuhr) A machine that copies an image and sends it to a computer.

video-conferencing (vih-dee-oh–KAHN-fuh-ruhn-sihng) Having a meeting with people in different places by means of audio and video signals.

visual (VIH-zhuh-wuhl) Having to do with sight or illustration.

INDEX

A
application, 9, 10, 12, 14, 15, 17, 19, 22, 30
audio, 4, 5, 16, 22

C
ChartGo, 20
collaborate, 6, 24

D
digital tools, 8, 9, 30
Dropbox, 25

F
Facebook, 10, 28

G
Gaggle, 10
Glogster, 8
Google Drive, 25
Google Hangouts, 24
Google Presentation, 8

I
infographics, 20, 21, 22, 25, 26, 27, 30
Instagram, 14

O
online community rules, 26

P
photographs, 4, 5, 12, 13, 14, 15, 22, 30
Picasa, 15
PicCollage, 14
Prezi, 8

S
safety, 28
Schoology, 10
Shutterfly, 15
Skype, 24
Snapfish, 15
social media, 10, 11, 15, 19, 20, 28

T
text, 4, 14, 16, 25
Tumblr, 10
Twitter, 10

V
video-conferencing, 24
videos, 4, 5, 6, 8, 10, 16, 18, 19, 26, 27, 30
Vimeo, 18

W
writing, 4, 6, 9, 10, 22, 25

Y
YouTube, 4, 10, 18

WEBSITES

Due to the changing nature of Internet links, PowerKids Press has developed an online list of websites related to the subject of this book. This site is updated regularly. Please use this link to access the list: www.powerkidslinks.com/cosk/expr